Ready for My Calling!
(formerly titled *Elder and Deacon Devotions*)

by

Rev. David A. Kahler

CDK Ministries^{SM}
Wyoming
2018

Ready for My Calling!
(formerly titled *Elder and Deacon Devotions*)
by Rev. David A. Kahler

Copyright © 2009, 2018 Rev. David A. Kahler. Originally published in 2009 under the title *Elder and Deacon Devotions*.

All rights reserved.

Published by CDK Ministries, LLC, Wyoming; CDKMinistries.com

"CDK Ministries" is a service mark of CDK Ministries, LLC.

Second Edition.

Cover photograph by Aaron Burden on Unsplash

ISBN 978-1-7325371-0-1 (paperback)
ISBN 978-1-7325371-1-8 (ebook)

Printed in the United States of America

DEDICATION

*To the 2 C's of CDK,
I'm absolutely Crazy about you!*

CDK MINISTRIES℠ AND KINGDOM PRICING

CDK Ministries exists to promote the Christian faith, making a positive impact in the lives of those ministered to, all with integrity of heart. To that end, it is more important to promote God's Kingdom than capitalize on His ministry.

God has called and inspired CDK Ministries' President, Rev. David A. Kahler, to get His Word into as many hearts as His Holy Spirit will allow. Therefore, the nominal price of this publication was set to cover the costs of printing, distribution, and other book industry charges. Less than 5¢ of this book's money goes to the author and publisher. This was done with Kingdom intentionality. This book was never written to make money; it was written to equip leaders of the church.

Still God's Word says, "You shall not muzzle an ox when it treads out the grain," and, "The laborer deserves his wages." (1 Timothy 5:18). If you have been equipped by this book and are able to give, please consider contributing a "gratuity" to the ministry. CDK Ministries is purposely set up to be a dynamic, streamlined ministry and therefore did not acquire non-profit status. Under the LLC structure, you cannot give a tax-deductible gift or donation, but you can give a gratuity; it is still NOT tax-deductible, but it does provide a way to perpetuate and multiply this ministry through which God spoke to you. Please consider going to CDKMinistries.com and giving a gratuity today.

If you'd like to have Rev. David A. Kahler speak at your church and/or next ministry event, please call or email him using the contact information on the website CDKMinistries.com.

The Lord bless you!

TABLE OF CONTENTS

INTRODUCTION .... - 1 -
PRAYERS FOR DEVOTIONAL TIME .... - 1 -
   A Prayer for the Opening of a Church Board Meeting...................... - 1 -
   A Prayer for the Close of a Church Board Meeting .... - 2 -
   A Prayer for a Meeting of the Elders.. - 2 -
   A Prayer for a Meeting of the Deacons .... - 2 -
A HELPFUL STUDY HINT .... - 3 -

ETYMOLOGY OF ELDER .... - 4 -

CHARACTER OF AN ELDER .... - 6 -

WISDOM OF AN ELDER .... - 7 -

PERSONAL CONDUCT OF AN ELDER .... - 8 -

THE ULTIMATE EXAMPLE FOR AN ELDER .... - 9 -

ELDER AS AN OFFICE .... - 10 -

RESPONSIBILITY OF AN ELDER .... - 11 -

THE TASK OF AN ELDER .... - 12 -

"ELDER, SHEPHERD THE FLOCK!" .... - 13 -

ELDERS AS HEALERS THROUGH PRAYER .... - 14 -

ELDERS AS HEALERS THROUGH ANOINTING WITH OIL .... - 16 -

ELDERS AS WORSHIP LEADERS .... - 18 -

ELDERS AS WITNESSES .... - 19 -

THE ANOINTING UPON ELDERS .... - 20 -

HONORING ELDERS .... - 21 -

ACCUSATIONS AGAINST ELDERS .... - 22 -

ETYMOLOGY OF DEACON .... - 23 -

CHARACTER OF A DEACON .... - 24 -

MORE CHARACTER OF A DEACON .... - 25 -

DEACON AND DEACONESS .... - 26 -

THE TASK OF A DEACON .... - 27 -

CALLING & ORDINATION OF ELDERS & DEACONS .... - 28 -

ELDERS, DEACONS, AND THE CHURCH .... - 30 -

THE OFFICES IN THE BELGIC CONFESSION, ART. 30 .... - 32 -

THE OFFICES IN THE BELGIC CONFESSION, ART. 31 .... - 33 -
WHAT'S NEXT? .... - 34 -

FROM THE AUTHOR

Introduction
      This book was written for the sole purpose of transforming its readers. You'll notice that each exercise requires you to name a task to do and a timeframe to do it in. It's because the book is meant to be more than informational; it's meant to be transformational. With that in mind, spend time reflecting on the questions and write down honest answers. Take time to truly ponder God's Word and how it applies to your life, setting realistic goals so that God may keep working His grace in you and to those around you.

Prayers for Devotional Time
Some uses for this book include:

- Personal devotions/study
- Opening devotions for church leadership meetings
- Elder/Deacon ordination preparation classes
- Small group studies on the church offices, church polity, and church leadership (i.e. - Adult Sunday Schools, Youth Small Groups, etc.)
- College and Seminary classes as part of the required reading for a church polity class

For those wishing to use this booklet for personal or corporate devotions, a great prayer to end with is the Lord's Prayer, not spoken as if racing to finish it, but meditated upon to give time for your heart, mind, body, and soul to speak. For those wishing to use this booklet as devotions for church leadership meetings, here are some more prayers to begin meetings with:

A Prayer for the Opening of a Church Board Meeting
Almighty and eternal God, who by Your Holy Spirit presided in the council of the Apostles in Jerusalem, and who promised through Your Son Jesus Christ to be with Your Church to the end of the world, we pray You to be with the consistory here assembled in Your name. Save us from all error, ignorance, pride

and prejudice. And of Your great mercy be pleased, we pray You, to direct, sanctify, and govern us in our work by the power of the Holy Spirit. Grant, O Lord, that those responsibilities committed to us may be discharged to Your glory, and that Your kingdom may be advanced in this place, until we all come to the fullness of eternal life; through the merits and death of Jesus Christ our Savior. Amen. (adapted from *Liturgy and Psalms*, New York: the Board of Education of the Reformed Church in America, 1968.)

A Prayer for the Close of a Church Board Meeting
O Lord God and Heavenly Father, we thank You that You have been pleased to establish this church and to use our service therein. We ask You to bless what we have done in Your name, and carry forward Your own work in our midst; that Your people may be built up on their most holy faith and that sinners may be converted to You; through Jesus Christ Your beloved Son. Amen. (adapted from *Liturgy and Psalms, ibid.*)

A Prayer for a Meeting of the Elders
Merciful God and Father, You rule and overruled at the council of the blessed Apostles, give us, as elders of this church, wisdom and guidance for its spiritual oversight. May our favor and influence with the people come from following Christ and not from worldly appeal. Guide our deliberations, we ask, and direct our motives, that our thoughts, words, and actions in this meeting may be according to Your holy will. Grant that Your Church may be strengthened, and Your name glorified in the midst of Your people; through Jesus Christ our Lord. Amen. (adapted from *Liturgy and Psalms, ibid.*)

A Prayer for a Meeting of the Deacons
Merciful God and Father, endow us deacons with wisdom. Enable us to distribute with all cheerfulness and fidelity the offerings of Your people for the well-being of Your Church and the coming of Your Kingdom. Strengthen us that we may faithfully perform all the duties to which You have called us. Grant us the grace to comfort those who are in need, not merely with gifts but also with Your Holy Word. And be pleased to

continue Your blessing over us, that all Your people may have reason to praise You, knowing the grace of our Lord Jesus Christ, that though He was rich, yet for our sakes He became poor, that we through His poverty might be rich. Amen. (adapted from *Liturgy and Psalms, ibid.*)

A Helpful Study Hint

If you come across a devotion that is about an office which you are not ordained to, try rewording the questions to fit your context. For example, a deacon reading the following question pertaining to an elder:

> What specific tasks will you do to fulfill the command in Acts 20:28 with your church?

may try to reword the question to:

> What specific tasks would you do to fulfill the command in Acts 20:28 with your church if you were an elder?

This would help you understand all the offices of the local church and give you a better understanding of their respective callings.

I pray you continue to grow up in every way into Jesus Christ, the head of you and the Church.

God bless you,

Rev. David A. Kahler

Etymology of Elder

- Read Acts 20:17, 28 and Titus 1:5,7

    In these passages, there are 2 different words used for elders. The word derived from πρεσβύτερος (*presbyteros*), where we get the English word *presbytery*, means someone older, an elder, a community leader. The word derived from ἐπίσκοπος (*episkopos*), where we get the English word *Episcopal*, means guardian, supervisor, keeper, church leader, overseer, bishop. The words are used separately in Scripture, but in Titus 1 and in Acts 20, the two are used interchangeably to describe the role of an ordained Elder. We have since used the definitions to devise whole systems of governing the church. You have the Episcopal system which is a hierarchal governing structure of popes, bishops, ministers, and church leaders. This system is employed by the Catholic, Episcopalian, and United Methodist denominations to name a few. And you have the Presbyterian system used by Presbyterians and Reformed Protestants, whereby the board of elders, including the minister, governs the church.

1. Looking at the roles of an elder through the above definitions of presbyteros and episkopos (*someone older, an elder, a community leader, guardian, supervisor, keeper, church leader, overseer, bishop*), which role do you feel most comfortable fulfilling?

2. Which role do you feel least comfortable fulfilling?

3. Who or what might equip you to fulfill that least comfortable role?

4. When will you begin seeking out that resource to equip you?

Character of an Elder

- Read 1 Timothy 3:1-7

    These verses talk about the character of an elder. While elders have different personalities, gifts, and abilities, all elders will have 1 Timothy 3's qualities in common. It's these features that distinguish an elder from the rest of the flock and support his true spiritual authority to govern over God's people.

1. Looking at the characteristics of an elder in 1 Timothy 3:1-7, which trait(s) do you feel you exemplify best?

2. What have others said to confirm your conclusion?

3. God is constantly working on our character. Sometimes it is a very intense working, and sometimes it is very mild. What characteristic do you sense God improving in you right now?

4. What can you do to further this character work within you?

5. When will you do it?

Wisdom of an Elder

- Read Job 12:13&20

    Job has been afflicted by Satan at the permission of God, yet his friends are sure it is because he has sinned. Job is correcting his friends in these verses, and in so doing, gives us insight into where wisdom lies in regards to elders.

1. With whom are wisdom and might?

2. Who has counsel and understanding?

3. Who takes away the discernment of the elders?

4. How can you gain more wisdom? (see also James 1:5-8)

5. Do you need to ask God for more wisdom?

6. If yes, then when will you do this?

Personal Conduct of an Elder

- Read Titus 1:5-9

    In order for an elder to be appointed a steward over God's flock, he must first demonstrate that he is a good steward over his own life. Elders give instruction to God's people and rebuke them according to His Word. An elder's personal and family conduct and character can support this ministry if it reflects a life in Christ, the Living Word. This is why it is so important for elders to be above reproach.

1. Comparing the overall conduct of your current life to Titus 1:5-9, what character traits do you display best?

2. What character traits would your fellow elders say you display best?

3. What trait needs the most work?

4. What will you do to improve that area of conduct?

5. When will you start improving that area?

The Ultimate Example for an Elder

- Read 1 Peter 2:13-25, especially verse 25

    Peter correlates submission to authority with a life in Christ Jesus. He gives Christ's own submission as the example for the way we should submit to authority. He then alludes that Christ's submission enabled Him to become Lord, the Supreme Overseer. From this we infer that our Christ-like submission to earthly, spiritual, and heavenly authority has and will enable us to become godly elders.

1. Name a time when an authority unjustly punished you.

2. Verse 24 mentions how God can use personal hurts to heal others. How has or how can God use your unjust experience with an authority to heal others?

3. Name an authority to whom you now submit.

4. In what ways are you following Christ's example to submit to that authority?

5. In what ways are you not?

6. Pray right now for God to empower you with the God-honoring submission of Jesus Christ.

Elder as an Office

- Read 1 Timothy 3:1

> The word for overseer, ἐπισκοπή (*episkopē*), in 1 Timothy 3:1 is not translated to overseer but to *office of overseer*. It is also translated to *visitation* as in God visiting humans. An office in the Church is an appointment, in every sense of the word, from God to His people with all its power to bless and punish. Church officers (ministers, elders, and deacons) visit, inspect, and provide for God's children with divine power and, depending on the investigation, bless, comfort, rebuke, and/or restrain with divine authority.

1. How do you feel about the divine authority and power you have been given in your office?

2. What can you do to ensure that you are executing your office with God's power to bless and punish?

3. How often will you do this while installed in your office? *[Note: ordination is forever. Installation is for a period of service.]*

4. How often will you do it throughout your ordination? *[Note: ordination is forever. Installation is for a period of service.]*

Responsibility of an Elder

- Read Acts 20:17-38; especially verse 28

    In his conversation with the board of elders in Ephesus, the Apostle Paul gives a command to them in verse 28. Notice the context in the verses before and after Acts 20:28 and how it shapes the command. Explore the following questions about Acts 20:28.

1. To whom are the elders to pay careful attention to, or over whom are the elders to keep watch?

2. Who makes overseers?

3. What do overseers do?

4. How did God obtain possession of the Church?

5. What specific tasks will you do to fulfill the command in Acts 20:28 within your church?

6. When will you complete those tasks? Or, if they are ongoing duties, how often will you perform them?

The Task of an Elder

- Read 1 Peter 5:1-4

> Elders are told to shepherd the flock, with certain parameters, looking ultimately to the chief Shepherd, Jesus Christ.

1. While elders can be paid (perhaps a preaching elder or pastor), they should not be motivated to shepherd the flock for exorbitant amounts. And while it is their duty to exercise oversight, begrudging obligation should not be their motivation to carry out that duty. According to verse 2, what is to be the motivation of the elder for shepherding the flock?

2. Elders have the God-given authority to oversee the flock, yet God calls them not to use an authoritarian style of leadership but one that is more sacramental in nature. Looking at verse 3, how are elders to lead those under their charge?

3. What is the reward for those who do these things until Christ comes back?

4. What in your leadership style or motivation do you need to change in order to conform more to 1 Peter 5:1-4?

5. How will you do it?

6. When will you do that?

"Elder, Shepherd the Flock!"

- Read 1 Peter 5:1-2 and Psalm 23.

> Psalm 23 is a poem that uses the metaphor of shepherding to illustrate God's Providence. With that in mind, it can be a cross reference in understanding the task of the elder to shepherd the flock. Elders lead their churches through change from old ministry to renewed ministry. They feed their congregation by teaching God's word to them. They discipline church members. Elders' leadership, teaching, and discipline feeds, refreshes, restores, edifies, comforts, and consecrates the people under their charge.

1. Which aspect of shepherding do you do best: leadership, teaching, or discipline?

2. Which aspect needs the most work?

3. With God's help, how will you strengthen that aspect?

4. When will you do that?

Elders as Healers through Prayer

- Read James 5:13-18

> In these verses, themes of the supernatural (supernatural healing, controlling the rain, eternal forgiveness of sins) are explored in relation to prayer. Followers of Jesus are to pray in all circumstances, whether suffering or cheerful. Elders are specifically called to pray for the sick. In this day and age where sickness is more attributed to germs and imperfect hygiene, we forget the nuances of this passage. The tradition of saying "God bless you" to folks who sneeze was solidified by the 8th century, but it proceeded from biblical thought that illness was because of sin or the devil. It would be unwise to entirely dismiss illness from spiritual forces as simply superstition, if indeed we believe the Holy Bible to be God's Word. Prayer and faith, especially of those called to the office of elder, can heal, can resurrect, and can absolve. "The prayer of a righteous person has great power as it is working."

1. Whose responsibility is it to seek healing prayer?

2. Who does the healing?

3. What do the elders' prayers save the sick from? (see also Matthew 18:18-20)

4. Do you believe that you, as an elder, have more power, to heal and to save, than the non-ordained?

5. Name some ways you can improve your belief in your God-given power as outlined in James 5:13-18?

6. How soon will you do it?

Elders as Healers through Anointing with Oil

- Read James 5:14

        Oil was used to anoint people and objects (Exodus 30:22-33). It set them apart. It made them holy. People that were anointed in Old Testament times were the priests and kings (1 Samuel 10:1 & 16:13).
        Oil is a ceremonial substance that establishes a special relationship between God and that which is being anointed, as in the wedding ceremony of Israel and God in Ezekiel 16:9. The elder, just like each disciple in Mark 6:13, is an agent of God that uses the anointing oil to establish a special relationship between God and the sick, thus to spare them from evil.

1. Whose responsibility is it to seek healing prayer?

2. Who does the healing?

3. How does it make you feel to know that you are an agent of God, given the power to establish special relationships between God and his people who are sick?

4. Do you believe that you as an elder have a more distinct function to heal and to save than the non-ordained?

5. Name some ways you can improve your belief in your God-given function to heal as outlined in James 5:14?

6. How soon will you do it?

Elders as Worship Leaders

- Read Revelation 4-5; 11:15-19; 19:1-10

    Notice the role the elders play in worshipping God in these passages, especially Revelation 4:4,10; 5:6,8,14; 11:16; & 19:4.

1. In what ways do the elders lead worship in these passages?

2. In what ways do you lead worship?

3. What do you need to do to conform more to God's Word as stated in Revelation 4,5,11,&19?

4. How soon will you do that?

Elders as Witnesses

- Read Matthew 18:15-20; see also Deuteronomy 21:1-9, 18-21; 22:13-21; 25:5-10

    Elders act as witnesses in the discipline process. They hear the arguments between two parties and help them resolve their issue according to God's Holy Word.

1. When are elders to enter into the discipline process?

2. Who is it that gets the elders involved?

3. What can you do to improve your congregation's discipline process towards Matthew 18:15-20?

4. How can you get the elder board and congregation to work towards that improvement?

5. When will you do it?

The Anointing Upon Elders

- Read Numbers 11:16-17, 24-25

    Moses was not able to carry his people all by himself, especially after their last grumbling for meat. In his prayer, he asked for a solution. God anointed elders.

1. How did the Lord anoint the elders?

2. What evidence was there that elders were anointed?

3. Whom do you have to help you bear the burden of the people?

4. What can you do to work with them so that you do not have to bear the burden alone?

5. How soon will you do it?

Honoring Elders

- Read 1 Timothy 5:17-18

    Paul uses Deuteronomy 25:4 (which he also uses in 1 Corinthians 9:9) and quotes Jesus as can be read in Luke 10:7 to support the command to give double honor. While all elders govern the church, some toil further in studying, teaching, and preaching the Word of God. It's especially these who are to be given double honor in the form of respect, wages, housing, food, etc.

1. Name three specific things your congregation does to give double honor to elders, especially those who teach and preach?

2. What can you do to enhance your church's giving double honor to elders, especially those who preach and teach?

3. When will you do that?

Accusations Against Elders

- Read 1 Timothy 5:19

    Satan uses a number of ways to slow down the church in making disciples. Accusing is one such way. In fact, the word Satan means accuser. Still there might be warrant to a charge against a fellow brother or sister in Christ, hence this passage.

1. How much evidence do you need to charge an elder?

2. Outline the basic procedure your church follows in handling a charge against an elder. (If you don't know it, find out now! Don't wait until it's too late.)

Etymology of Deacon

- Read 1 Timothy 3:8-13

> In this passage two forms of the word deacon are used, διάκονος (*diakonos*), which is found in 1 Timothy 3:8&12, and διακονέω (*diakoneō*), which is found in 1 Timothy 3:10&13. The noun form of deacon, diakonos, means an official of the church entrusted to serve the needs of believers. The verb form of deacon, diakoneo, means to be a deacon, to minister unto. It also means to wait upon tables in Acts 6:2, which connotes to serve and handle finances.

1. Looking at the forms of a deacon through the above definitions of diakonos and diakoneo (*church official, servant, minister, waiter*), which role do you feel most comfortable fulfilling?

2. Which role do you feel least comfortable fulfilling?

3. Who or what might equip you to fulfill that least comfortable role?

4. When will you begin seeking out that resource to equip you?

Character of a Deacon

- Read 1 Timothy 3:8-13

    These verses talk about the character of a deacon. While deacons have different personalities, gifts, and abilities, all deacons will have 1 Timothy 3's qualities in common. It's these features that distinguish a deacon from the rest of the flock and support his stature as an ordained servant among God's people.

1. Looking at the characteristics of a deacon in 1 Timothy 3:8-13, which trait do you feel you exemplify best?

2. What have others said to confirm your conclusion?

3. God is constantly working on our character. Sometimes it is a very intense working, and sometimes it is very mild. What characteristic do you sense God operating on in you right now?

4. What can you do to further this character work in you?

5. When will you do it?

More Character of a Deacon

- Read Acts 6:3

    Notice the characteristics the apostles give in picking deacons.

1. What 3 characteristics are we to look for in picking deacons?

2. Which trait do you feel you best exemplify?

3. Which of these 3 traits do you need to work on the most?

4. What can you do to let God further this work in you?

5. When will you do it?

Deacon and Deaconess

- Read Romans 16:1

    Some translations use the word *servant* instead of *deaconess* in this verse. It is their way of dealing with the conflict of a female deacon against 1 Timothy 3:12, which calls a deacon to be the husband of one wife. But the conflict still exists because the word for deacon in 1 Timothy 3:12 and Romans 16:1 has both a male and female form. Some of the most reliable and oldest Greek translations use the female form for deacon in Romans 16:1, affirming female deacons in the early Church.

1. The conflict of women in leadership can be argued for and against using the same Word of God. What is your view of women in leadership?

2. What biblical arguments do you use to back up your stance?

3. How do you encourage women in ministry whether ordained or non-ordained?

4. What can you do to further this work?

5. When will you do it?

The Task of a Deacon

- Read Acts 6:1-7

These verses mark the beginning of the office of deacon, established to resolve a multitude of issues in the early Church and beyond. An injustice was going on between the Hebrews and the Hellenists. There was a distribution problem, not one of cash but of finances in the way of food. There was also a mercy problem in that some of the widows were being overlooked. There was a service problem as to who should be served. There was an outreach problem in that the Church's outreach was being impeded by this unresolved issue. There was also a missions problem due to the cross-cultural issue at hand. The office and task of deacon was created to resolve Church issues with injustice, finances, mercy, service, outreach, and missions.

1. What Church problems and issues do you address as a deacon?

2. What additional problems can you and other deacons tackle to improve fulfilling the command of our Lord to the Church to make disciples?

3. How can you tackle them?

4. Who can help?

5. When will you start tackling them?

Calling & Ordination of Elders & Deacons

- Study 1 Timothy 4:13-14; See also Acts 6:6 and Acts 14:23

    Paul recites the events of Timothy's ordination to encourage him in his ministry. Timothy was given the gift of preaching and teaching by prophecy and laying on of hands. Today we use the terms personal and corporate calling instead of the term prophecy, but they are similar. Both are inspired utterances, both involve a corporate response of the congregation in the ordination, and both require a personal acceptance of the divine utterance by the newly ordained person.

1. Can you recall the events that lead to your calling and ordination?

2. What did you spiritually sense?

3. What was God doing in the calling? (See 1 Corinthians 1:26-31 for more)

4. What was He doing in the ordaining? (See 2 Corinthians 1:21-22 for more)

5. How have you affirmed your calling and ordination into your office?

6. What can you do to re-affirm your calling and ordination into your office?

7. When will you do that?

Elders, Deacons, and the Church

- Read Philippians 1:1-2

    In the beginning of this letter to the Philippian Church, Paul and Timothy address the members and leaders of the Church there.

1. How do Paul and Timothy address the general congregation of Philippi?

2. How do they address the leaders?

3. Like the Triune God, the saints, overseers, and deacons are one in the Lord and yet each have a specific office, role, and function. What is your office, role, and function?

4. How are you distinct in your role and how are you one with your congregation?

5. How can you help others see (in love) your uniqueness and commonality?

6. When will you do this?

Use These Last 2 Creedal Devotions to Support Your Biblical Understanding of Elders & Deacons

The Offices in the Belgic Confession, Art. 30

- Read Article 30 of the Belgic Confession

    In a document that was meant to set the record straight with the Roman Catholic Church, who was accusing Protestants of straying from the Church, the writers give a creedal understanding of God's Word in regards to Elders and Deacons.

1. Who, together with Ministers of Word & Sacrament, form the council of the Church?

2. Applying what you have already read in this devotional, which office preserves the true religion, propagates true doctrine, chastens and restrains transgressors by spiritual means?

3. Which office relieves and comforts the poor and distressed, according to their necessities?

4. How can your church council better integrate its various offices, each with their distinct roles and tasks?

5. When will you do it?

The Offices in the Belgic Confession, Art. 31

- Read Article 31 of the Belgic Confession

1. Who is to be involved in the choosing of ministers, elders, and deacons?

2. Why should people wait and not force their calling?

3. Is one minister to be above another as in bishops, cardinals, and popes?

4. How are ministers and elders to be esteemed?

5. How can you aid the form of church government described in Article 31 of the Belgic Confession?

6. When will you do it?

What's Next?
A Ministry Journal

An additional way to grow in Church Leadership is to write about your ministry as an Elder or Deacon. Write down the date, who you helped, what you did, where it happened, why you did what you did, and how it made you feel. Refer back to your entries when you want to reflect on all that God has done through you, when you need a pick-me-up during those hard times of ministry, when you need to be reminded of your calling, or anytime you have a desire to go over your previous entries. Below are a couple of examples to help you if you are unsure as to what to write.

Example 1
We had a Deacons meeting on December 1, 2017. A congregant asked us for help in paying her mortgage. We voted to give her $1,000 from our Deacons Fund. I volunteered to help her find a Christian debt specialist for the long haul, and Suzie volunteered to contact her and offer her prayer support. I'm glad I can offer some help, and I pray God will get her out of this predicament.

Example 2
Sunday, March 1, 2018. I presented John and Jane Christian to the congregation to be baptized. I was nervous standing in front of all those people, and I was also thrilled to play a special part in the Sacrament.

CDK MINISTRIES℠ AND KINGDOM PRICING REVISTED

CDK Ministries exists to promote the Christian faith, making a positive impact in the lives of those ministered to, all with integrity of heart. To that end, it is more important to promote God's Kingdom than capitalize on His ministry.

God has called and inspired CDK Ministries' President, Rev. David A. Kahler, to get His Word into as many hearts as His Holy Spirit will allow. Therefore, the nominal price of this publication was set to cover the costs of printing, distribution, and other book industry charges. Less than 5¢ of this book's money goes to the author and publisher. This was done with Kingdom intentionality. This book was never written to make money; it was written to equip leaders of the church.

Still God's Word says, "You shall not muzzle an ox when it treads out the grain," and, "The laborer deserves his wages." (1 Timothy 5:18). If you have been equipped by this book and are able to give, please consider contributing a "gratuity" to the ministry. CDK Ministries is purposely set up to be a dynamic, streamlined ministry and therefore did not acquire non-profit status. Under the LLC structure, you cannot give a tax-deductible gift or donation, but you can give a gratuity; it is still NOT tax-deductible, but it does provide a way to perpetuate and multiply this ministry through which God spoke to you. Please consider going to CDKMinistries.com and giving a gratuity today.

If you'd like to have Rev. David A. Kahler speak at your church and/or next ministry event, please call or email him using the contact information on the website CDKMinistries.com.

The Lord bless you!

www.ingramcontent.com/pod-product-compliance
Lightning Source LLC
Chambersburg PA
CBHW060344080526
44584CB00013B/917